America's First Peoples

12588

the Shoshone

Pine Nut Harvesters of the Great Basin

by Kristin Thoennes Keller

Consultant:
Deward E. Walker Jr., Ph.D.
Professor of Anthropology
  and Ethnic Studies
University of Colorado, Boulder

Blue Earth Books

an imprint of Capstone Press
Mankato, Minnesota

Blue Earth Books are published by Capstone Press
151 Good Counsel Drive, P.O. Box 669, Mankato, Minnesota 56002
http://www.capstone-press.com

Library of Congress Cataloging-in-Publication Data
Thoennes Keller, Kristin.
    The Shoshone : pine nut harvesters of the Great Basin / by Kristin Thoennes Keller.
    v. cm.—(America's first peoples)
    Includes bibliographical references and index.
    Contents: The Great Basin Shoshone—The harvest—Pine nuts—The pine nut festival—The western Shoshone—The northern
Shoshone—The eastern Shoshone—The Shoshone today.
    ISBN 0-7368-2173-2 (hardcover)
    1. Shoshoni Indians—Food—Juvenile literature. 2. Shoshoni Indians—Social life and customs—Juvenile literature. 3. Pine nuts—Juvenile
literature. [1. Shoshoni Indians. 2. Indians of North America—Great Basin.] I. Title. II. Series.
E99.S4T46 2004
978.004'9745—dc21   2003001470
Summary: Discusses the Shoshone Indians, focusing on their tradition of harvesting pine nuts. Includes a recipe for apricot-pine nut muffins.

Editorial credits
Editor: Megan Schoeneberger
Series Designer: Kia Adams
Cover Production Designer: Jennifer Schonborn
Photo Researcher: Wanda Winch
Product Planning Editor: Karen Risch

Cover images: Shoshone woman with children in travois, Riverton
Museum; basket with pine nuts, University of Nevada-Reno Library,
Special Collections

Photo credits
balasart/Susan Balas-Whitfield, 27
Capstone Press/Gary Sundermeyer, 3 (all), 9, 13, 23
Corbis/Swift/Vanuga Images, 28–29
Idaho State Historical Society, 14–15, 17 (right), 22
Jackson Hole Historical Society and Museum/Helen Lang
    Collection/Henry E. Stamm, IV, Ph.D., 15 (right)

Marilyn "Angel" Wynn, 4 (left), 4–5, 7 (right), 18 (top), 21 (right),
    25 (right), 29 (right)
National Archives and Records Administration/Yellowstone
    National Park, 20–21
Nevada Historical Society, 8 (left), 10–11
Riverton Museum, 24–25
Smithsonian Institution/National Anthropological Archives,
    16–17, 26
University of Nevada-Reno Library, Special Collections, 11 (right)
U.S. Fish & Wildlife Service/John and Karen Hollingsworth, 19
Utah State Historical Society, used by permission, all rights
    reserved, 6–7
The Walters Art Museum, Baltimore, 12
Wyoming State Museum, 18 (bottom); Department of State Parks
    and Cultural Resources, 8 (right)

1 2 3 4 5 6 08 07 06 05 04 03

Contents

Chapter 1   The Great Basin Shoshone   4

Chapter 2   The Harvest   6

Chapter 3   Pine Nuts   10

Chapter 4   The Pine Nut Festival   14

Chapter 5   The Western Shoshone   16

Chapter 6   The Northern Shoshone   20

Chapter 7   The Eastern Shoshone   24

Chapter 8   The Shoshone Today   28

Features

Words to Know   30

To Learn More   30

Places to Write and Visit   31

Internet Sites   31

Index   32

On page 9, learn to play a game called Hand-and-Stick.

Learn to make apricot-pine nut muffins on page 13.

Learn how to make bread beads on page 23.

Chapter One

The Great Basin Shoshone

Long ago, the Shoshone people roamed across a large area. This region is known as the Great Basin. It includes most of what is now Nevada. Parts of Utah, Oregon, Idaho, and California also make up the Great Basin.

Shoshone stories tell that a spirit named Coyote was the reason their people lived all over the Great Basin. Years ago, the creator placed two women on the land. The women asked a spirit

The Shoshone lived in small groups throughout the Great Basin.

named Coyote to carry a basket for them. They told Coyote not to open the basket, no matter what happened. But Coyote was too curious. He opened the basket again and again. Each time, people jumped out of the basket.

Food was the real reason early Shoshone people lived in different areas. Food sources were used up too quickly when many people lived together. The Shoshone moved around within certain areas to find food.

The Shoshone gradually broke into three main groups. They are known as the Western, Northern, and Eastern Shoshone. All three groups still think of themselves as one tribe.

Chapter Two

The Harvest

Many small Shoshone groups gathered in fall for the pine nut harvest. This event brought friends together. They saw each other only once a year.

The Shoshone found nuts in the pinecones of pinyon pine trees. Each scale of the cone held two pine nuts. In early fall, the cones turned brown. The color signaled that cones were ready for harvest.

Everyone had a job in the harvest. Some boys climbed trees to shake down the cones. Men knocked cones down with long poles. Other children gathered the cones into baskets. Girls and women carried the heavy loads back to the camp.

Several small Shoshone groups gathered in one large group to harvest pine nuts.

Basket Weaving

The Shoshone used baskets for many things. They covered some baskets with pitch. These baskets could hold water for cooking. Other baskets were used as roasting or gathering trays. Sometimes, the Shoshone used baskets as hats or fans. Cradleboard baskets helped women carry small babies.

Women made baskets during summer. They used plants and branches. Baskets were easy to carry. Shoshone women needed them as they moved around to find food.

Baskets covered with sticky pitch were waterproof.

7

A sticky substance called pitch covered the cones. In the cool morning air, the pitch was not as sticky. As the sun rose in the sky, its warmth melted the pitch. Pitch often covered the Shoshone's bodies at the end of the day. They sometimes rolled in dirt before bedtime. The dirt kept the pitch from sticking to their fur blankets.

Men, women, and children worked together to harvest pine nuts.

The Shoshone played many games to pass time when they were not hunting or gathering food. Shoshone adults and children played Hand-and-Stick with animal bones. You can play this Shoshone game using drinking straws.

Some game sticks the Shoshone used were made from wood.

Hand-and-Stick Game

What You Need

eight drinking straws
six or more people, evenly divided
    into two teams

What You Do

1. Divide players into teams A and B.
2. Give four straws to a player on Team A. Give four straws to a player on Team B.
3. Team A's members pass and pretend to pass their straws to one another. They use tricks to fool the other team. At the end of passing, all of Team A's players act as though they have the straws. They all fold their arms in front of them as if hiding something. Only one person holds all the straws.
4. Team B's players must guess who is holding the straws. If they guess right, they get one straw from Team A. If they guess wrong, they must give one straw to Team A.
5. Team B's members take turns passing and pretending to pass their straws. Team A takes turns guessing.
6. Play continues back and forth until one team runs out of straws. The team with all the straws wins.

Chapter Three

Pine Nuts

At the camp, women worked to get the nuts from the pinecones. They dug pits and lined them with rocks. They emptied baskets of cones into the pits. The women then covered the pits with dirt and lit fires. The fires' heat warmed the cones, opening them. The women carefully dug up the cones. They then pulled the nuts from the cones.

The women cooked the pine nuts in many ways. They dropped hot stones into a basket filled with water. The stones heated the water. The women added pine nuts to the hot water to soften them. Women also roasted pine nuts over an open fire.

Women and girls helped pick the pine nuts from the roasted cones.

Each scale of a cone held two pine nuts.

11

The Shoshone ate pine nuts throughout the year. They ate them whole and roasted, like peanuts. Women ground some pine nuts into flour. They used the flour to make mush or thick gravy. They ate this gravy with meats or stews. In winter, children ate frozen pine nut gravy as a treat. Women also made a thin soup out of pine nut flour. They added berries, leaves, and ground meat or fish to the soup.

The Shoshone prepared meals over a fire.

Apricot-Pine Nut Muffins

The Shoshone mostly used pine nuts in soups and gravies. Today, pine nuts are used in many recipes, such as these tasty muffins.

What You Need

Ingredients

2 cups (480 mL) flour
½ cup (120 mL) sugar
1 teaspoon (5 mL) baking soda
¼ teaspoon (1.2 mL) salt
1 cup (240 mL) plain yogurt
¼ cup (60 mL) milk
¼ cup (60 mL) butter or margarine, melted and cooled
1 egg, lightly beaten
2 tablespoons (30 mL) honey
1 teaspoon (5 mL) vanilla
¾ cup (175 mL) chopped dried apricots
½ cup (120 mL) pine nuts

Equipment

nonstick cooking spray
muffin pan
large mixing bowl
dry-ingredient measuring cups
measuring spoons
mixing spoons
medium mixing bowl
liquid measuring cups

What You Do

1. Preheat oven to 400°F (200°C). Spray muffin pan with nonstick cooking spray. Set aside.
2. In large mixing bowl, stir together flour, sugar, baking soda, and salt. Set aside.
3. In medium mixing bowl, stir together yogurt, milk, butter, egg, honey, and vanilla until blended.
4. Use a spoon to make a well in the center of the dry ingredients. Add yogurt mixture and stir to combine.
5. Stir in apricots and all but 2 tablespoons (30 mL) of the pine nuts.
6. Spoon batter into muffin pan. Sprinkle batter with remaining pine nuts.
7. Bake 15 to 20 minutes or until golden brown.

Makes about 12 muffins

Chapter Four

The Pine Nut Festival

The Shoshone celebrated the pine nut harvest with a festival each year. A man or woman acted as pine nut chief. This person started the festival by throwing a handful of pine nuts in each of the four directions. The pine nut chief thanked the creator for life and asked for a good harvest.

All members of the tribe joined in the festival. They said prayers together. People crossed their arms over their chests, gently striking themselves. They then raised their arms, bringing their hands together.

Finally, they opened their hands and blew between them. These actions symbolized cleansing their bodies.

Dancing was another part of the festival. People danced to thank the creator for the pine nuts. The festival lasted for weeks. It ended when all of the pine nuts were harvested.

Men wore their finest clothing for dances and festivals.

Shoshone Dancing

Dances were a large part of Shoshone religious life. The dances could be happy or sad, fast or slow. Some dances lasted for several days.

The Shoshone danced for many reasons. Often, the dancers gave thanks for their food. People danced to heal the sick, avoid illness, and change the weather. Shoshone people also danced to show sadness when a loved one died.

Chapter Five

The Western Shoshone

After the harvest, Shoshone groups returned to their winter camps. They would not see the other Shoshone groups until the next year's pine nut festival. For the rest of the year, the groups followed their own customs.

The Western Shoshone built cone-shaped homes from tree branches. They covered the branches with grass, leaves, and animal skins. These coverings kept the snow and cold out of the home. They built fires in the center of the home for cooking and for warmth.

Families shared a home made from branches and animal skins.

The Shoshone Name

Some neighboring American Indian tribes called the Shoshone "Rattlesnakes" or "Snakes." This name may have had something to do with Shoshone homes. They built shelters of branches, grass, and leaves. These homes probably reminded other tribes of snakes living in the grass.

Early groups of Shoshone had other names for themselves. Some called themselves Eaters of Groundhogs, Mountain Sheep Eaters, or Eaters of Salmon. Other names were Eaters of Jackrabbits, Eaters of Buffalo Grass, and Eaters of Wild Wheat. They also called themselves Pine Nut Eaters.

Today, the Shoshone people have two names for themselves. They call their people Newe or Nimi. These words mean "the people."

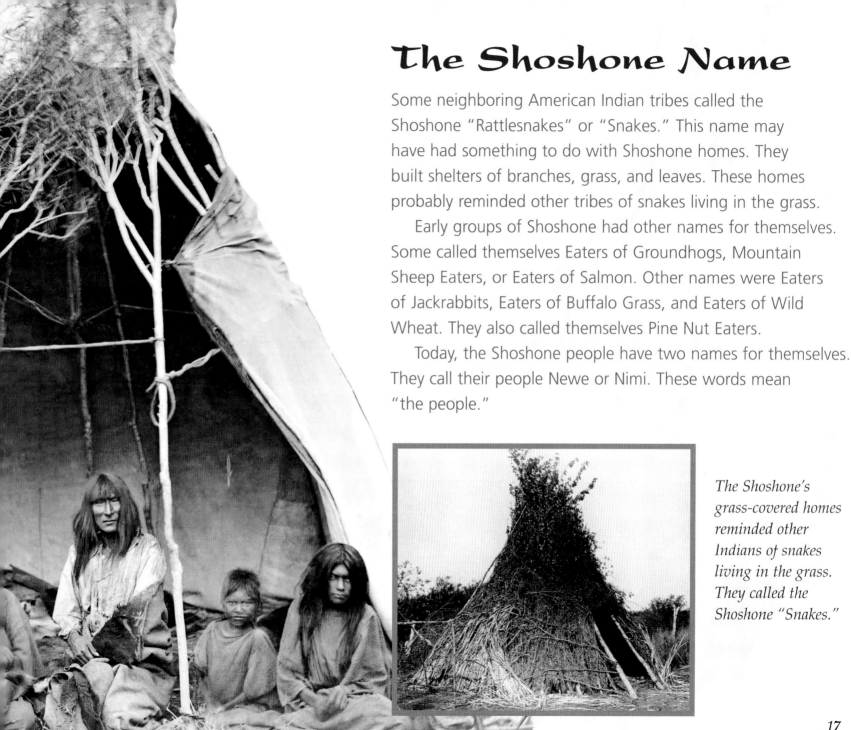

The Shoshone's grass-covered homes reminded other Indians of snakes living in the grass. They called the Shoshone "Snakes."

17

The Western Shoshone people enjoyed many foods besides pine nuts. During spring, men hunted groundhogs, birds, and other small animals. Women and children gathered fruits, seeds, leaves, and roots. In fall, men hunted rabbits, antelope, and deer.

Animals were used for more than meat. The Western Shoshone used rabbit fur to make clothing and blankets. Men made bowstrings from strips of animal skin. Bones made useful tools for cutting and scraping.

Winter was the time for storytelling. Many Shoshone stories told about a spirit named Coyote. This spirit was very curious and always getting into trouble. Children listened to the stories while warming their feet on heated rocks.

The Western Shoshone wore rabbit-fur clothing. They scraped the skins clean with tools made from animal bones.

The Legend of Coyote and the Pine Nuts

One time when Coyote was running along, snow swirled around him. The cold wind blew hard. He could not see where he was going.

Coyote could run no more. He stopped to rest and fell asleep. As snow piled up around him, Coyote nearly froze to death. But he did not notice. He dreamed he was sleeping next to a warm fire.

Coyote woke in an old man's house. He was very sick. The kind old man fed him soup to make Coyote stronger.

Day after day, Coyote ate the tasty soup. Coyote grew stronger. But he pretended to be sick so he could eat more soup.

After many months, Coyote grew curious. One morning, he followed the old man to a pile of pinecones beneath a group of pine trees. Coyote watched as the old man gently struck the cones. Nuts fell from the cones. The old man then ground the nuts into powder. He added water to the powder to make soup.

The next morning after breakfast, Coyote told the old man that he was ready to go home.

Coyote pretended to leave. But he secretly followed the old man to the cones. He waited all day.

When the old man left, Coyote grabbed a bag and began to stuff it with cones. He filled the bag until it became very heavy. It dragged on the ground as Coyote started toward home.

Coyote did not know that the old man had cut a tiny hole in the bag. As the bag dragged on the ground, the hole grew. Cones spilled out. Coyote did not notice the bag becoming lighter. He was thinking of all the delicious nuts he would eat when he got home. By the time Coyote was home, he had lost most of the cones. These cones grew into large trees scattered across the Great Basin.

Chapter Six

The Northern Shoshone

The Northern Shoshone did not eat as many pine nuts as the other groups ate. Salmon was the most important food for the Northern Shoshone. Men used harpoons or traps to catch these fish. Each spring, the people celebrated the salmon.

Northern Shoshone also hunted. They used bows and arrows to kill deer, antelope, mountain sheep, and buffalo. Most men rode horses to hunt buffalo. Some men wore the skins of antelope as a costume. In the costume, they walked close to the buffalo herd. The buffalo were not frightened. When the hunters got close enough, they shot their arrows.

Hunters on horseback surrounded a buffalo herd. Horses were able to keep up with the running herd.

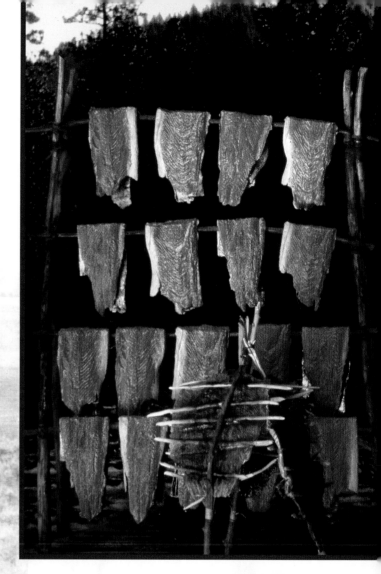

Salmon meat was hung on racks to dry. Dried fish and other meat lasted for many months without spoiling.

21

The Northern Shoshone also ate roots and berries. Women dug the roots of the camas flower during summer. Camas roots were sweet. Shoshone women sometimes boiled them to make a sweet tea. They also dried the roots and mashed them to make flour for cooking.

The Northern Shoshone made clothing from the animals they hunted. They wore buffalo robes in winter. They wore deerskin clothing in summer. They made their shoes from animal skins.

A woman filled her basket with camas roots. She carried the basket on her back as she returned home.

Make Bread Beads

Shoshone women sewed tiny beads onto clothing to create colorful designs. They decorated vests, dresses, and pouches. The earliest designs were squares, diamonds, stripes, and triangles. One Shoshone bead design is the Shoshone Rose.

You can make your own beads. They will not be as tiny as the beads the Shoshone used on their clothing. You can use your beads to make a necklace or wristband.

What You Need

slice of white bread with the crust removed

paper cup

white school glue

plastic spoon

round toothpicks

poster paint in your favorite colors

paintbrush

yarn or string

What You Do

1. Tear the slice of bread into very small pieces. Put them into the paper cup.
2. Add three spoonfuls of white glue to the bread.
3. Carefully stir the sticky mixture.
4. Scoop the mixture from the cup. Work it around in your hands to make a smooth ball of dough.
5. Pull small pieces of dough off the ball.
6. Roll each piece of dough into a small bead.
7. Make a hole through the center of each bead with a toothpick.
8. Allow the beads to dry overnight.
9. Paint the beads with poster paints. Allow the paint to dry.
10. Thread yarn or string through the beads to make a necklace or wristband.

Chapter Seven

The Eastern Shoshone

The Eastern Shoshone also used buffalo, mountain sheep, and deer for meat and skins. The men hunted on horses while the women butchered and dried the meat.

The Eastern Shoshone had many uses for animal skins. One Eastern Shoshone tepee needed at least 10 buffalo hides. Like the Northern Shoshone, the people wore buffalo robes in winter. In summer, they wore deerskin clothing.

Meat hung on ropes strung between tepees to dry.

Beaded designs decorated deerskin
dresses and other clothing.

25

Everyone in the Eastern Shoshone groups had their own job. Women gathered berries and roots. They took care of the children and made baskets, clothing, and tepees. Older girls gathered twigs and branches for the fire. They helped the women with cooking and cleaning. Older boys took care of the horses. Eastern Shoshone men made shields, drums, and rattles from parts of the buffalo.

Women and girls used many types of baskets to gather food and twigs.

Who Was Chief Washakie?

Washakie was born in the early 1800s. As an infant, he was named Pina Quanah, which meant "smell of sugar."

He earned the name Washakie in battle. Before joining a fight, he made a large rattle with stones inside a buffalo skin balloon. He attached the rattle to a stick and shook it at the enemy's horses. The horses were frightened by the loud noise. His tribe gave him his new name, which meant "the rattle."

As a leader, Chief Washakie became known for his wisdom in dealing with the U.S. government. Chief Washakie helped the Eastern Shoshone get some of their land back from the United States. He asked the U.S. government to pay for Shoshone land it did not return. He asked the U.S. government to build schools, churches, and hospitals on Shoshone land.

Chief Washakie is remembered for his battle skills and his leadership.

Chapter Eight

The Shoshone Today

Today, many Shoshone people live on reservations in the Great Basin. Each reservation has schools, libraries, stores, banks, and gas stations. The people live modern lifestyles.

The Shoshone still try to preserve some old ways of life. Every year, the Shoshone have a fall pine nut festival. They work hard to keep their language, traditions, and culture alive.

Shoshone children learn about their culture by attending festivals and other gatherings.

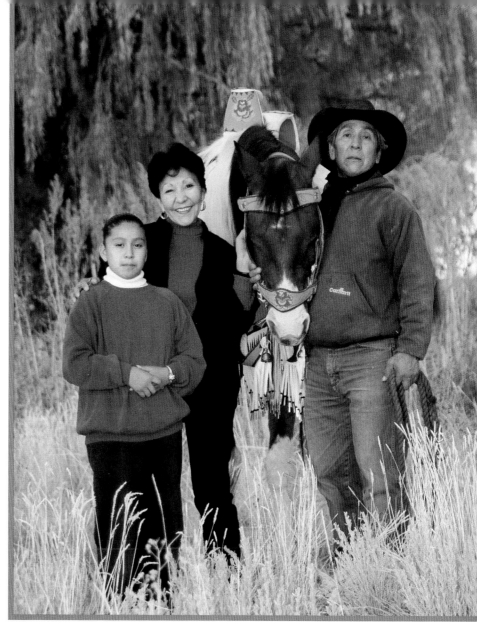

Shoshone families carry on
some traditions while living
a modern lifestyle.

Words to Know

camas (KAM-us)—a flower belonging to the lily family

festival (FESS-tuh-vuhl)—a celebration that is held at the same time each year

harvest (HAR-vist)—to collect or gather crops that are ripe; the food that is gathered is sometimes called the harvest.

pinyon pine (pin-YON PINE)—a tree that grows in the western United States and produces cones containing pine nuts

pitch (PITCH)—a sticky substance that covers the cones of a pinyon pine tree

reservation (rez-ur-VAY-shuhn)—land that the U.S. government sets aside for an American Indian nation to use

scale (SKALE)—one of the small pieces that cover the outside of a pinecone

tradition (truh-DISH-uhn)—a custom, belief, or idea that is passed on to younger people by older relatives or tribal members

To Learn More

Ansary, Mir Tamim. *Great Basin Indians.* Native Americans. Des Plaines, Ill.: Heinemann Library, 2000.

Bial, Raymond. *The Shoshone.* Lifeways. New York: Benchmark Books, 2001.

Blackhawk, Ned. *The Shoshone.* Indian Nations. Austin, Texas: Raintree Steck-Vaughn, 2000.

Mattern, Joanne. *The Shoshone People.* Native Peoples. Mankato, Minn.: Bridgestone Books, 2001.

Places to Write and Visit

Antelope Valley Indian Museum

15701 East Avenue M

Lancaster, CA 93534

National Museum of the American Indian

4220 Silver Hill Road

Suitland, MD 20746

Eastern Shoshone Culture Center

First Street

Fort Washakie, WY 82514

Shoshone Bannock Tribal Museum

IH 15

Fort Hall, ID 83203

Internet Sites

Want to find out more about the Shoshone?
Let FactHound, our fact-finding hound dog, do the research for you.

Here's how:

1) Visit *http://www.facthound.com*
2) Type in the **Book ID** number: **0736821732**
3) Click on **FETCH IT.**

FactHound will fetch Internet sites picked by our editors just for you!

www.FactHound.com
SM

Index

animal skin, 16, 18, 20, 22, 24, 25, 27

basket, 5, 6, 7, 10, 22, 26
beads, 23, 25
buffalo, 20, 21, 22, 24, 26, 27

clothing, 15, 18, 22, 23, 24, 25, 26
cooking. See food
Coyote, 4–5, 18, 19
creator, 4, 14, 15

dancing, 15

Eastern Shoshone, 5, 24, 26, 27

families, 16, 29
festival, 14–15, 16, 28

food, 5, 7, 8, 15
  berries, 12, 22, 26
  fruits, 18
  meat, 12, 17, 18, 21, 24
  pine nuts, 6, 7, 8, 10, 11, 12, 13, 14, 15, 17, 18, 19
  roots, 18, 22, 26
  salmon, 17, 20, 21
fur, 8, 18

games, 8
Great Basin, 4–5, 19, 28

harvest, 6, 7, 8, 14–15
home, 16, 17, 24, 26
hunting, 18, 20, 21, 24

language, 28

Newe, 17
Nimi, 17
Northern Shoshone, 5, 20, 22, 24

pinecones, 6, 8, 10, 11, 19
pine nut chief, 14
pitch, 7, 8

scale, 6, 11
Shoshone Rose, 23
stories, 4–5, 18, 19

tepee. See home

Washakie, Chief, 27
Western Shoshone, 5, 16, 18